W9-CZS-305

># Mary Engelbreit's ⚬<
"Bountiful Harvest"

Edited by Jill Wolf
Text copyright © 1994
Antioch Publishing Company
ISBN 0-7824-8041-1

Printed in the U.S.A.

Note: Some measurements in parentheses
are British Imperial measure.

>👁 Mary Engelbreit's 👁< "Bountiful Harvest"

Art by Mary Engelbreit
Edited by Jill Wolf

 Antioch Publishing Company
Yellow Springs, Ohio 45387

A good deed is never lost;
he who sows courtesy reaps friendship,
and he who plants kindness gathers love.

—St. Basil

❧ CONTENTS ☙

Broccoli-Cheese Bites

3 tbsp. (2 ¼ Br. tbsp.) butter
1 ¼ lb. fresh broccoli
3 eggs, well-beaten
1 cup (8 fl. oz.) all-purpose flour
1 cup (8 fl. oz.) milk
1 tsp. (¾ Br. tsp.) salt
1 tsp. (¾ Br. tsp.) baking powder
1 lb. grated cheddar cheese
2 tbsp. (1 ½ Br. tbsp.) finely chopped onion

Preheat oven to 350° F. Melt butter in a 9 x 13 baking dish. Steam broccoli until partially cooked. Chop finely in a blender or food processor. Beat eggs thoroughly in a large bowl. Add flour, milk, salt, and baking powder. Mix thoroughly, then stir in cheese, broccoli, and onion. Spoon mixture into baking dish. Spread evenly. Bake until set, about 30 to 35 minutes. Let stand for 5 minutes before cutting into bite-size pieces. Serve.

Some people like to make a little garden
out of life and walk down a path.
— Jean Anouilh

WHO LOVES A GARDEN
STILL HIS EDEN KEEPS

ME A.B.ALCOTT

9

Mushrooms Mediterranean

1 lb. mushrooms
1 cup (8 fl. oz.) olive oil
1 cup (8 fl. oz.) dry white wine
$\frac{1}{2}$ tsp. salt
$\frac{1}{4}$ tsp. pepper
$\frac{1}{4}$ tsp. garlic powder
1 tbsp. ($\frac{3}{4}$ Br. tbsp.) lemon juice
1 tsp. ($\frac{3}{4}$ Br. tsp.) grated lemon rind

Put all ingredients in a saucepan. Bring to a boil.
Simmer for 15 minutes. Chill. Skewer mushrooms with
serving picks. Serve with a little of the sauce.

Melon and Prosciutto

Cut a ripe cantaloupe or honeydew melon into bite-
size pieces. Wrap each piece with a strip of thinly sliced
prosciutto or Virginia ham. Secure with a serving pick.

But with every deed you are sowing a seed,
Though the harvest you may not see.
—Ella Wheeler Wilcox

Herbed Tomato Soup

$^1/_4$ cup (2 fl. oz.) olive oil
2 medium onions, chopped
4 medium tomatoes, chopped
2 tsp. (1 $^1/_2$ Br. tsp.) dried basil
a pinch each of thyme, marjoram, oregano,
    and garlic powder
1 tbsp. ($^3/_4$ Br. tbsp.) fresh parsley, chopped
$^1/_2$ tsp. salt
$^1/_4$ tsp. black pepper
3 cups (24 fl. oz.) water

Heat oil in a large saucepan over medium heat. Sauté
onions in oil until lightly browned. Add the tomatoes.
Cook for 5 more minutes. Raise heat to high. Add
remaining ingredients. Bring to a boil. Reduce heat to
medium. Cook soup for 15 minutes. Puree soup in
small batches in a blender or food processor. Return
soup to pot. Reheat to a boil over high heat and serve.

*Cheerfulness is the atmosphere in which
all things thrive.*
—Jean Paul Richter

Vichyssoise

2 tbsp. (1 ½ Br. tbsp.) butter
3 medium leeks, finely chopped
1 medium onion, finely chopped
4 medium potatoes, peeled and thinly sliced
4 cups (32 fl. oz.) chicken stock
1 cup (8 fl. oz.) cream
salt and pepper to taste
chopped fresh watercress or chives

Heat butter in a large saucepan over medium heat. Sauté the leeks and onion in butter for about 5 minutes. Add the potato slices and chicken stock. Cover pan and simmer until potatoes are tender (about 15 minutes). Put soup through a ricer, blender, or food processor in small batches. Return to saucepan. Add cream. Season with salt and pepper. Serve hot or very cold, garnished with watercress or chives.

Wise sayings often fall on barren ground;
but a kind word is never thrown away.
—Sir Arthur Helps

Vegetable Soup

1 tbsp. (³/₄ Br. tbsp.) olive oil
1 medium onion, chopped
2 stalks celery, chopped
1 large bell pepper, chopped
4 cups (32 fl. oz.) chicken stock
2 cups (16 fl. oz.) chopped tomatoes
2 carrots, cut in rounds
3 medium potatoes, cut in cubes
¹/₈ tsp. garlic powder
¹/₄ tsp. each: thyme, basil, pepper, oregano,
    and marjoram

Heat oil in a large saucepan over medium heat. Sauté onion, celery, and bell pepper in oil for about 5 minutes. Add the stock, remaining vegetables, and seasonings. Bring soup to a boil. Reduce heat, then simmer until vegetables are tender (about 20 to 25 minutes).

Let us cultivate our garden.
    —Voltaire

Spinach-Mushroom Salad

$^1/_4$ *lb. fresh spinach*
$^1/_2$ *lb. fresh mushrooms*
1 cup (8 fl. oz.) cauliflower florets
a dozen or more cherry tomatoes
$^1/_2$ *cup (4 fl. oz.) blue cheese dressing*

Wash all vegetables and let drain, leaving mushrooms until the last. Put spinach into a large salad bowl, tearing off any tough stems. Add cauliflower florets. Slice the mushrooms into salad. Cut tomatoes in half and add. Toss salad with dressing and serve.

You can put everything . . . into salad . . .
but everything depends upon the skill of mixing.
—Charles Dudley Warner

Watercress Salad

$1/_4$ lb. watercress
4 ounces water chestnuts
8 to 12 radishes
6 tbsp. (4 $1/_2$ Br. tbsp.) salad oil
2 tbsp. (1 $1/_2$ Br. tbsp.) lemon juice
2 tsp. (1 $1/_2$ Br. tsp.) sesame oil
2 tsp. (1 $1/_2$ Br. tsp.) toasted sesame seed
salt and pepper to taste

Clean watercress; remove thicker stems. Arrange on salad plates. Slice the water chestnuts and arrange on top of watercress, then do the same with the radishes. Shake the remaining ingredients in a covered glass jar, mixing thoroughly. Pour over salads and serve.

*To own a bit of ground, to scratch it with a hoe,
to plant seeds and watch the renewal of life—
this is the commonest delight . . .*
—Charles Dudley Warner

IF YOU PRAY FOR RAIN, BE PREPARED TO DEAL WITH SOME MUD.

17

Zucchini Salad

1/2 lb. small zucchini
1/4 cup (2 fl. oz.) olive oil
3 tbsp. (2 1/4 Br. tbsp.) lemon juice
1/4 tsp. dried oregano
1/8 tsp. garlic powder
1/4 tsp. black pepper
Parmesan or feta cheese

Scrub zucchini thoroughly. Cut off the ends and slice the zucchini very thin. Arrange zucchini on salad plates. Shake the remaining ingredients, except for the cheese, in a covered glass jar. Drizzle the dressing over the salads. Grate the cheese and sprinkle over the salads. Serve immediately.

A garden is not for giving or taking.
A garden is for all.
—F. H. Burnett

Potato Salad with Parsley

3 lbs. red or white potatoes, scrubbed, cooked, and
   drained
1 tbsp. (³/₄ Br. tbsp.) white wine vinegar
1 cup (8 fl. oz.) diced peeled cucumber
2 cups (16 fl. oz.) cooked green peas
1 cup (8 fl. oz.) finely chopped onion
¹/₂ cup (4 fl. oz.) coarsely chopped parsley or watercress
1 cup (8 fl. oz.) light mayonnaise
1 tbsp. (³/₄ Br. tbsp.) prepared white horseradish
1 tbsp. (³/₄ Br. tbsp.) white wine vinegar
1 tbsp. (³/₄ Br. tbsp.) chopped fresh dill
¹/₄ tsp. white or black pepper

Cut warm potatoes into cubes. Place in a large glass
bowl. Sprinkle with the one tbsp. of vinegar. Let cool,
then add the cucumber, peas, onion, and parsley.
Combine remaining ingredients to make dressing;
pour over salad and toss. Cover and chill before
serving.

Goodness is the only investment that never fails.
                                    —Henry David Thoreau

19

Pasta Primavera Salad

8 ounces rotini
2 cups (16 fl. oz.) broccoli florets
1 cup (8 fl. oz.) thinly sliced zucchini
1 cup (8 fl. oz.) asparagus, cut into 1-inch pieces
1/2 cup (4 fl. oz.) chopped onion
1/4 cup (2 fl. oz.) olive oil
2 cups (16 fl. oz.) cherry tomatoes, cut in halves
2 tbsp. (1 1/2 Br. tbsp.) minced fresh parsley
1/2 cup (4 fl. oz.) bottled creamy-style Italian dressing
1/2 cup (4 fl. oz.) grated Parmesan cheese
1/4 cup (2 fl. oz.) milk

Cook rotini, following directions on package. Drain well. Sauté the broccoli, zucchini, asparagus, and onions in the oil until tender, but not browned. Add tomatoes and parsley. Simmer for 5 minutes. Whisk together the dressing, cheese, and milk in a small bowl until smooth. Combine pasta, vegetable mixture, and dressing in a large salad bowl; toss lightly. Garnish with more parsley and Parmesan, if desired, and serve.

Work—for some good, be it ever so slowly;
Cherish some flower, be it ever so lowly . . .
—Frances Sargent Osgood

Snow Pea Salad

1 lb. fresh snow peas
$^1/_2$ lb. fresh mushrooms, sliced
$^3/_4$ cup (6 fl. oz.) sliced scallions
$^1/_2$ cup (4 fl. oz.) sliced water chestnuts
$^1/_4$ cup (2 fl. oz.) salad oil
2 tbsp. (1 $^1/_2$ Br. tbsp.) vinegar
2 tsp. (1 $^1/_2$ Br. tsp.) soy sauce
$^1/_8$ tsp. garlic powder
$^1/_4$ tsp. ground ginger
$^1/_4$ tsp. ground pepper

Remove ends and strings from pea pods. Bring enough salted water to cover peas to boil in a saucepan. Add peas and cook for 2 minutes. Do not overcook—peas should be crisp. Drain and cool. Toss with mushrooms, scallions, and water chestnuts in a salad bowl. Shake remaining ingredients in a covered glass jar. Pour over salad and serve.

Who loves a garden still his Eden keeps,
Perennial pleasures plants, and wholesome
harvests reaps.
—Amos Bronson Alcott

Grapefruit-Avocado Salad

2 grapefruit, white or pink
2 avocados*
1 small onion
crisp salad greens
4 tbsp. (3 Br. tbsp.) lime or lemon juice from concentrate
4 tbsp. (3 Br. tbsp.) honey
4 tbsp. (3 Br. tbsp.) sour cream
$^1/_4$ tsp. celery seed

Peel grapefruit and section into slices, then pare avocado and cut into small wedges. Slice onion into very thin rings. Arrange the salad greens on serving plates. Place grapefruit sections, avocado wedges (or apple slices) and onion rings on top of greens. In a bowl whisk together the remaining ingredients, then drizzle over salads and serve.

* You may substitute slices of unpared red apple for the avocado and omit the onion.

Where there is hatred, let me sow love . . .
—St. Francis of Assisi

SOW GOOD SERVICES;
SWEET REMEMBRANCES
WILL GROW FROM THEM.

Mde. de Stael

24

Melon-Cucumber Salad

4 tbsp. (3 Br. tbsp.) salad oil
2 tbsp. (1 ¹/₂ Br. tbsp.) lemon juice
1 tsp. (³/₄ Br. tsp.) sugar
¹/₄ tsp. salt
¹/₄ tsp. pepper
2 small cucumbers, thinly sliced
1 cup (8 fl. oz.) watermelon cubes
1 cup (8 fl. oz.) honeydew melon cubes
¹/₄ cup (2 fl. oz.) chopped celery
large lettuce leaves

Whisk the first five ingredients together in a large
salad bowl. Add the remaining ingredients except for
the lettuce. Toss the salad with the dressing. Arrange
lettuce on serving plates. Transfer salad to lettuce on
serving plates with a slotted spoon.

One should learn also to enjoy the neighbor's
garden, however small . . .
—Henry van Dyke

Waldorf Salad

1 cup (8 fl. oz.) diced unpared red apples
1 cup (8 fl. oz.) diced unpared yellow apples
2 tbsp. (1 ¹/₂ Br. tbsp.) lemon juice
1 cup (8 fl. oz.) halved seedless green grapes
1 cup (8 fl. oz.) halved seedless red grapes
¹/₂ cup (4 fl. oz.) chopped celery
¹/₄ cup (2 fl. oz.) chopped walnuts
1 cup (8 fl. oz.) mayonnaise or mayonnaise-like dressing

Toss diced apple with lemon juice in a large salad bowl.
Add grapes, celery, and nuts. Blend mayonnaise thoroughly into salad. Chill before serving.

. . . to know someone who thinks and feels with us . . .
and is close to us in spirit, this makes the earth
for us an inhabited garden.
—*Johann Wolfgang von Goethe*

The heart of the giver makes the gift dear & precious

·LUTHER·

27

Pear and Cheese Salad

4 ripe pears
2 tbsp. (1 ¹/₂ Br. tbsp.) lemon juice
leaf lettuce
¹/₄ cup (2 fl. oz.) lemon juice
¹/₄ cup (2 fl. oz.) sugar
2 tbsp. (1 ¹/₂ Br. tbsp.) dry sherry
¹/₂ cup (4 fl. oz.) shredded Gouda cheese or crumbled
    Roquefort cheese
¹/₄ cup (2 fl. oz.) chopped pine nuts or walnuts

Pare, core, and slice pears. Toss slices with the two tbsp.
lemon juice to prevent discoloration. Arrange lettuce
on serving plates, then place pear slices on top. Stir
sugar slowly into the ¹/₄ cup lemon juice. Add sherry.
Drizzle dressing over pears, then sprinkle with cheese
and nuts. Serve immediately.

I ask not for a larger garden,
But for finer seeds.
—Russell Conwell

 **SIDE DISHES**

Tomatoes and Zucchini

¹/₂ cup (4 fl. oz.) chopped onion
1 tbsp. (³/₄ Br. tbsp.) corn oil or olive oil
1 lb. sliced zucchini
2 cups (16 fl. oz.) chopped peeled tomatoes
1 tsp. (³/₄ Br. tsp.) oregano
¹/₈ tsp. garlic powder
1 tsp. (³/₄ Br. tsp.) salt
¹/₄ tsp. pepper

Sauté onion in oil in a skillet with a lid. Stir in the zucchini and tomatoes, then season with oregano, garlic, salt, and pepper. Cover and cook over low heat for about 10 to 15 minutes, or until tender. Serve in bowls.

■ ■ ■ ■ ■ ■ ■ ■ ■ ■ ■ ■ ■ ■ ■

Happiness is not having what you want,
but wanting what you have.
—Hyman Schachtel

GIVE US THIS DAY OUR DAILY BREAD

Sautéed Potatoes

2 lbs. small red potatoes
6 tbsp. (4 ½ Br. tbsp.) olive oil
½ cup (4 fl. oz.) chopped onion
1 medium green or red bell pepper, sliced into thin strips

Scrub potatoes. Boil until tender. When potatoes are
cool, cut into quarters. In a large skillet sauté the
onion and pepper slices in olive oil over medium heat
until tender. Add potatoes. Sauté potatoes, stirring
gently, until heated through and coated with oil.

*Remember this: that very little is needed
to make a happy life.*
—Marcus Aurelius

Seasoned "Fries"

2 lbs. white potatoes
1/4 cup (2 fl. oz.) olive oil
ground black pepper
ground paprika

Preheat oven to 400° F. Peel and wash potatoes. Pat dry with paper towels. Cut potatoes lengthwise into 1/2-inch slices. Cut slices again into thin strips. Place strips on a pair of non-stick surface baking sheets, drizzle with oil, and toss to coat. Spread out strips on sheets, then sprinkle generously with pepper and paprika. Bake in oven for 20 minutes. Take out; cool potatoes for 5 minutes. Return to oven for about 10 minutes, until potatoes are lightly browned. Serve immediately.

Be glad of life because it gives you the chance to love and to work and to play and to look up at the stars . . .
—Henry van Dyke

Grilled Vegetables

mushroom caps
zucchini wedges
potato slices
eggplant slices
carrot wedges
pieces of bell pepper
small tomatoes or tomato halves
small whole onions, parboiled
parboiled corn cobs, cut into 1-inch rings
salad oil, seasoned with salt and pepper

Spear a selection of vegetables on skewers. Brush with seasoned oil. Barbecue over medium coals until cooked, turning frequently. Baste with more oil if necessary. Serve hot.

There is time for work. And time for love.
That leaves no other time.
—Coco Chanel

ONE TOUCH of NATURE MAKES THE WHOLE WORLD KIN. SHAKESPEARE

34

Vegetable Stir-Fry

2 tbsp. (1 ½ Br. tbsp.) olive oil or vegetable oil
1 small onion, chopped
2 stalks celery, thinly sliced crosswise
2 large leaves Chinese cabbage, thinly sliced crosswise
2 cups (16 fl. oz.) small broccoli florets
1 medium green or red bell pepper, chopped
¼ lb. snow peas
½ cup (4 fl. oz.) water chestnuts, sliced
½ cup (4 fl. oz.) sliced mushrooms
¼ tsp. pepper
⅛ tsp. garlic powder
2 cups (16 fl. oz.) chicken broth
2 tbsp. (1 ½ Br. tbsp.) cornstarch
white or brown rice
soy sauce

Heat oil over medium-high heat in large, heavy skillet or wok. Stir-fry the vegetables for about 5 minutes, seasoning with pepper and garlic; reduce heat if necessary. Remove vegetables from pan to large platter. Pour chicken broth in pan. Slowly stir in cornstarch and cook mixture on medium-high heat until thickened. Stir in vegetables until just reheated. Serve over rice with soy sauce.

A weed is but an unloved flower!
— Ella Wheeler Wilcox

Green Beans with Almonds

1 lb. fresh green beans
1/2 cup (4 fl. oz.) water
2 tbsp. (1 1/2 Br. tbsp.) butter
1/4 tsp. salt
4 tbsp. (3 Br. tbsp.) slivered, toasted almonds

Wash beans. Remove ends. Cut into 1-inch pieces.
Cook and stir all ingredients except almonds in a
saucepan over medium heat until butter is melted.
Cover; cook 20 to 25 minutes or until beans are tender.
Stir in almonds. Serve.

I want it said of me . . . that I always . . . planted a
flower where I thought a flower would grow.
—Abraham Lincoln

Lemon Asparagus

1 1/2 lbs. fresh asparagus
5 tbsp. (3 3/4 Br. tbsp.) butter
1/4 cup (2 fl. oz.) water
2 tsp. (1 1/2 Br. tsp.) lemon juice
1/2 tsp. salt
1/4 tsp. pepper

Break off tough end of asparagus stalks. Wash asparagus. Remove tough scales. Cut each stalk diagonally into 1-inch pieces. In large skillet heat butter, water, and juice to boiling. Add asparagus, salt, and pepper. Cover. Cook over medium-high heat for 5 to 8 minutes or until asparagus is tender but crisp. Do not overcook. Serve immediately.

Life's field will yield as we make it
A harvest of thorns or of flowers.
—Johann Wolfgang von Goethe

Glazed Baby Carrots

1 lb. baby carrots
juice of one lemon
1 tsp. ($^3/_4$ Br. tsp.) honey
1/2 tsp. ground ginger or nutmeg
1 tbsp. ($^3/_4$ Br. tbsp.) butter

Peel carrots. Bring an inch of water to boil in a 2 $^1/_2$-quart saucepan. Add carrots. Cook on medium-high heat until tender. Drain. Set aside in a bowl. In the saucepan, combine remaining ingredients. Heat and stir. Add carrots and cook on high heat for about a minute, shaking the pan constantly. Serve.

Happiness is itself a kind of gratitude.
—Joseph Wood Krutch

Strawberry Soup

1 quart fresh strawberries
2 tbsp. (1 ¹/₂ Br. tbsp.) white wine
1 cup (8 fl. oz.) plain yogurt
1 cup (8 fl. oz.) lemon yogurt

Wash and hull berries. Pat dry with a paper towel.
Blend ingredients in a blender or food processor until
smooth. Serve in dessert cups or bowls.

For everything you have missed,
you have gained something else.
—Ralph Waldo Emerson

41

Carrot Bread

3 extra large eggs
1 3/4 cup (14 fl. oz.) sugar
1 cup (8 fl. oz.) vegetable oil
3 cups (24 fl. oz.) all-purpose flour
1 tsp. (3/4 Br. tsp.) baking soda
1 tsp. (3/4 Br. tsp.) salt
1/2 tsp. baking powder
2 tsp. (1 1/2 Br. tsp.) nutmeg
one half of a lemon, cut in half and with seeds removed
2 cups (16 fl. oz.) finely shredded raw carrots

Beat the eggs in a large mixing bowl. Add the sugar gradually, beating until thick. Blend in oil gradually, until thoroughly mixed. Sift together the flour, baking soda, salt, baking powder, and nutmeg. Stir flour mixture into egg mixture until smooth. Grind the unpeeled lemon quarters in a blender or food processor. Add ground lemon and shredded carrots to flour-egg mixture; stir until well blended. Pour into two well-greased 5 x 9 loaf pans, filling each two-thirds full. Bake at 350° F for about 50 minutes or until cake tester inserted in center of loaves comes out clean.

Then give to the world the best you have,
And the best will come back to you.
—Madeline Bridges

Fruit and Cheese Tray

Serve a selection of three to four cheeses and seasonal fresh fruit as the dessert course for a luncheon or dinner. Allow cheese to come to room temperature before serving. Arrange cheeses on a wooden cheese board, marble slab, or cheese platter. Garnish with grape leaves, cress, or parsley. Provide cheese cutters, scoops, small knives, and dessert plates. Place fruit on a fancy tray, plate, or lazy susan. Or, arrange both fruit and cheese on a large tray. If desired, serve with an assortment of unsalted crackers and a dessert wine, such as port, cream sherry, Marsala, Madeira, or Tokay.

Suggested fruits: apples, pears, grapes, plums, peaches, strawberries, apricots, pineapple

Cheese combinations: Brie, Port du Salut, and Emmenthaler; Camembert, Provolone, and Cheddar; Bel Paese, Cheddar, Stilton, and Samsoe; Liederkranz, Gouda or Edam, and Danablu; Gloucester, Gorgonzola, and Gruyère or Fontina; Gjetöst, Colby, Emmenthaler, and Roquefort; Alsatian Muenster, Chévre, and Cheshire

The reward of a thing well done is to have done it.
—Ralph Waldo Emerson

Grapes in Wine

1/2 lb. green seedless grapes
1/2 lb. red seedless grapes
1/4 cup (2 fl. oz.) dry white wine
1/4 cup (2 fl. oz.) sweet white wine
2 tbsp. (1 1/2 Br. tbsp.) sugar
1/4 tsp. ground ginger

Place grapes in four small dessert dishes. Combine remaining ingredients in a glass measuring cup; pour wine mixture over fruit. Chill and serve.

Try these other combinations as a light dessert: Four peeled and sliced fresh pears with a mixture of 1/4 cup (2 fl. oz.) honey and 1/4 cup (2 fl. oz.) sauterne, or four peeled and sliced fresh peaches with 3 tbsp. (2 1/4 Br. tbsp.) sugar and 1/2 cup (4 fl. oz.) rosé. Add a pinch of ginger to the pear or peach combinations, if desired.

Life is a flower of which love is the honey.
—Victor Hugo

Raspberry Dream

1 cup (8 fl. oz.) fresh raspberries
1 pint (16 fl. oz.) softened vanilla ice cream
1 tsp. ($^{3}/_{4}$ Br. tsp.) lemon juice

Mix all ingredients in a blender until smooth.
Pour into glasses or dessert cups. Serve with
dessert spoons and cocktail straws.

What sunshine is to flowers, smiles are to humanity.
—Joseph Addison

HURT NOT THE EARTH, NEITHER THE SEA, NOR THE TREES.

REVELATIONS 7:3

Mary Engelbreit is an internationally recognized artist and designer whose work combines warmth, wit, nostalgia, and a unique style. Born and raised in a suburb of St. Louis, Missouri, her artistic talent surfaced early. Though mostly self-taught, Mary attended summer art classes after high school. After a few years working as a commercial illustrator, Mary signed a short contract with Portal Publications, where she quickly established a national reputation. In 1986, Mary sold the rights to publish her greeting cards to Sunrise Publications. Since that time she has developed a strong licensing program. Mary Engelbreit designs appear on a wide variety of products, including tins, mugs, plates, Christmas ornaments, picture frames, clothing, and home textiles. Mary lives in St. Louis with her husband and their two sons.